For Bowie – C.S.

*For my family and friends,
for accompanying me during this trip – X.A.*

BIG PICTURE PRESS

First published in the UK in 2018 by Big Picture Press,
an imprint of Kings Road Publishing,
of the Bonnier Publishing Group,
The Plaza, 535 King's Road, London, SW10 0SZ
www.templarco.co.uk/big-picture-press
www.bonnierpublishing.com

1 3 5 7 9 10 8 6 4 2

ISBN 978-1-78741-074-9

This book was typeset in Ulissa and BSKombat.
The illustrations were created with graphite,
wax and ink, and coloured digitally.

Designed by Winsome d'Abreu and Olivia Cook
Edited by Joanna McInerney
Published by Lisa Edwards

Printed in Malaysia

The Speed
of Starlight

Written by **COLIN STUART**

Illustrated by **XIMO ABADÍA**

B P P

PHYSICS

SOUND

LIGHT AND COLOUR

SPACE

Welcome to the Universe

Our Universe is a truly remarkable place, rivalling even the most vivid imagination. There are worlds with two sunsets, planets where it rains diamonds and skies filled with so many stars that it never gets dark. As vast galaxies smash together, their stars spin dizzyingly out into the lonely void of space.

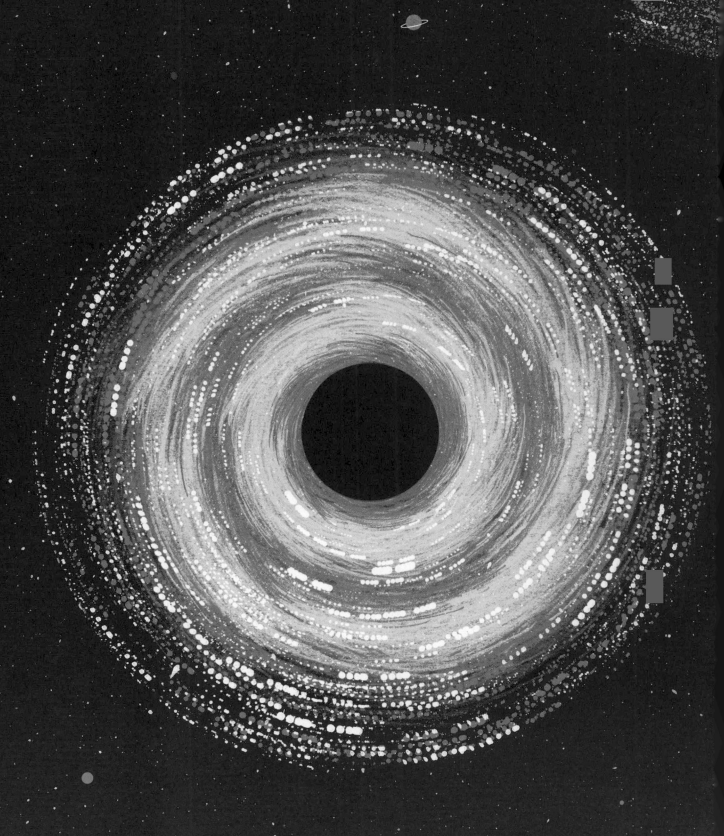

BLACK HOLES twist and warp not only space but time, too. **STARS** explode with such unimaginable force that they can outshine the light of a billion of their neighbours combined.

A dying star can become so squeezed that a single teaspoon of it weighs more than every person on the Earth put together.

The **SUN** has magnetic mood swings which see it belch out **a billion tonnes of gas** hurtling across the Solar System at more than a million kilometres per hour. Icy **COMETS** plunge close to the Sun's inferno as country-sized **ASTEROIDS** tumble silently around it.

But there is one thing as remarkable as the beauty of the Universe – our ability to understand it. Science, and in particular physics, has allowed us to peek behind the curtain and discover how the Universe works.

What is Physics?

Physics is the science of **ENERGY**, **MATTER** and **FORCES**. Think of it like a cookbook for the cosmos. It contains all the ingredients – the forces and particles – needed to make everything around us. It even tells us how to combine them together in different ways to explain why objects behave the way they do. Physics explains everything from an electric circuit to the birth of our Universe.

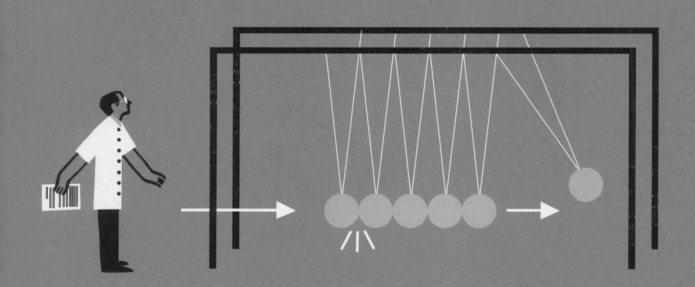

Physics can be divided into two main sets of rules – **QUANTUM PHYSICS** for the **very small** and Einstein's **GENERAL THEORY OF RELATIVITY** for the **very big**. Physicists would love to combine these two theories together to create one huge 'Theory of Everything', but so far that has proved very difficult to do.

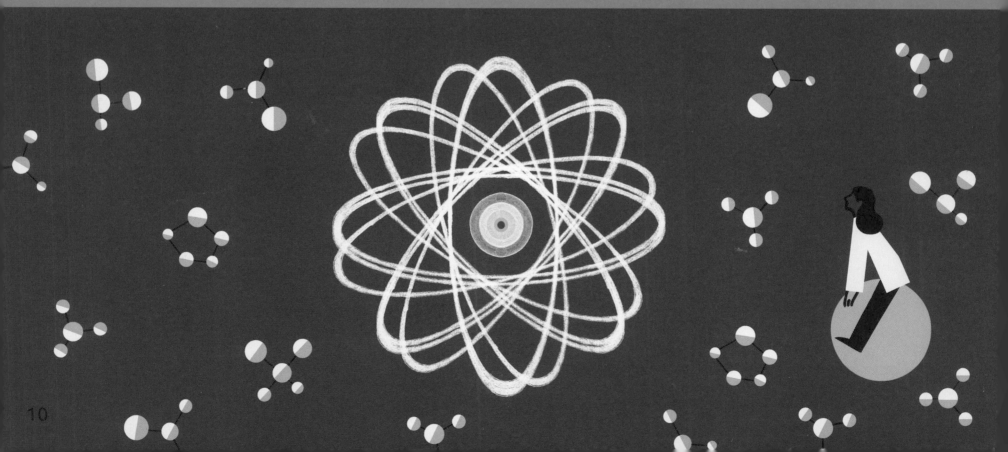

There are also some bits of the Universe that physicists don't currently know how to explain. For example, there seems to be an invisible glue holding galaxies together called dark matter (page 71), but we don't know what it is made of. So physics is just as much about trying to solve new mysteries as successfully explaining old ones. Physics is never finished.

Newton's Laws of Motion

A person who studies physics is called a **physicist** and ISAAC NEWTON is one of the most famous physicists of all time. He did very important work on forces – when an object pushes or pulls on another.

He not only came up with a theory about the force of gravity, he also put together three rules for **how objects move**. They are called NEWTON'S THREE LAWS OF MOTION.

LAW ONE

Unless a force is acting, a stationary object will remain stationary and an object travelling at a constant speed will continue at that speed in the same direction.

LAW TWO

The more force you apply to an object, the more it accelerates.

100kg

100

LAW THREE

For every action there is an equal and opposite reaction.

These laws of motion help us send rockets into space. To get a stationary rocket moving we need to **first apply a force [LAW ONE]. LAW TWO** tells us **how much force** we need to apply and **LAW THREE** tells us **where we need to apply it**. So, for the rocket to take off, we need to fire something out of the bottom of it.

Down to Earth

Nearly four kilometres above the surface of the Earth you jump out of a plane. As you hurtle towards the ground the wind rushes past your ears and the sound is deafening. Then you open your parachute and everything falls silent as you drift towards a safe landing.

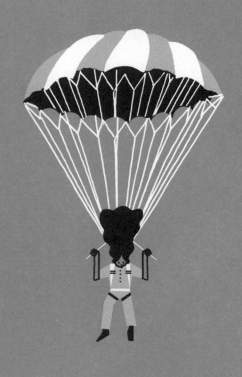

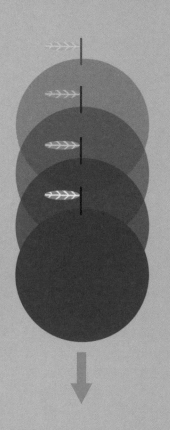

Skydivers fall to Earth because there is six thousand million million million tonnes of planet pulling them down. Isaac Newton's genius was to realise that the Moon orbits the Earth for the same reason an apple (or a skydiver) falls – an attractive force called GRAVITY. This is the **invisible force that pulls objects towards each other**.

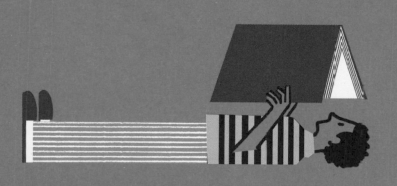

If any two objects have a gravitational attraction towards each other, then that means you are gravitationally attracted to this book. So why aren't you being pulled closer to it? Well, the strength of the gravitational force is not enough to overcome the force of FRICTION between the book and your hands. Friction is **the force that slows down objects which rub against each other**.

WHY DOESN'T THE MOON FALL DOWN?

Actually the Moon is always falling, but it is moving at such a perfect speed, that it continually circles the Earth. Any faster, and it would shoot off into space, any slower and it would crash into us! Gravity is also what holds all the planets in our Solar System in orbit around the Sun.

Electricity
and
Magnetism

CRASH! BANG! BOOM! As a thunderstorm rages and rumbles overhead, suddenly a fork of lightning tears towards the Earth and lights up the sky. This is nature at its fiercest and is an impressive display of the power of electricity.

ELECTRICITY is a type of energy that comes from the **flow of electric charge**. When **electric charges move** they also create something else – **MAGNETISM**. Electricity and magnetism are so closely related that physicists describe them both with one force – the **ELECTROMAGNETIC FORCE**. It is stronger than gravity which is why you can lift up one magnet with another.

electromagnetic force

gravity

Without magnetism you wouldn't be here. The Earth has a giant **MAGNETIC FORCE FIELD** around it thanks to **electrical charges moving around inside our planet's molten core**. This shield deflects a lot of particles coming down from space that are dangerous to living things. It's one of the reasons sending people to Mars is difficult – once you're out of our friendly magnetic field you have to invent a new way to protect astronauts, such as building protective pods.

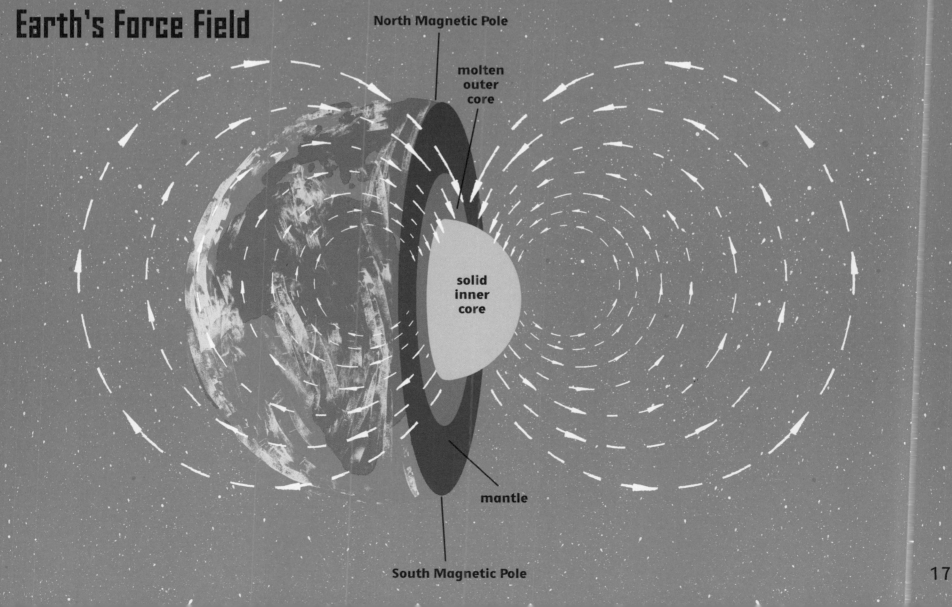

Earth's Force Field

North Magnetic Pole

molten
outer
core

solid
inner
core

mantle

South Magnetic Pole

Inside the Atom

Everything we see around us is made up of **tiny building blocks** called **ATOMS**. In your body alone there are several billion billion billion of them. In the whole Universe, we think there are one with 80 zeroes after it! It looks like this:

100, 000, 000, 000, 000, 000, 000, 000, 000, 000, 000, 000, 000, 000, 000, 000, 000, 000, 000, 000, 000, 000, 000, 000, 000, 000, 000, 000.

The Atom

You can think of an atom as a bit like a mini version of the Solar System. There is a **NUCLEUS in the centre** in place of the Sun and **negatively charged ELECTRONS** whizzing around the outside like little planets.

Inside the nucleus you'll find **positively charged PROTONS** along with **NEUTRONS** which **have no charge**. The electrons stay stuck to the nucleus because they are attracted to the protons by the electromagnetic force.

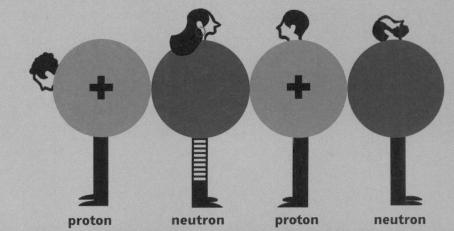

electron   proton   neutron   proton   neutron

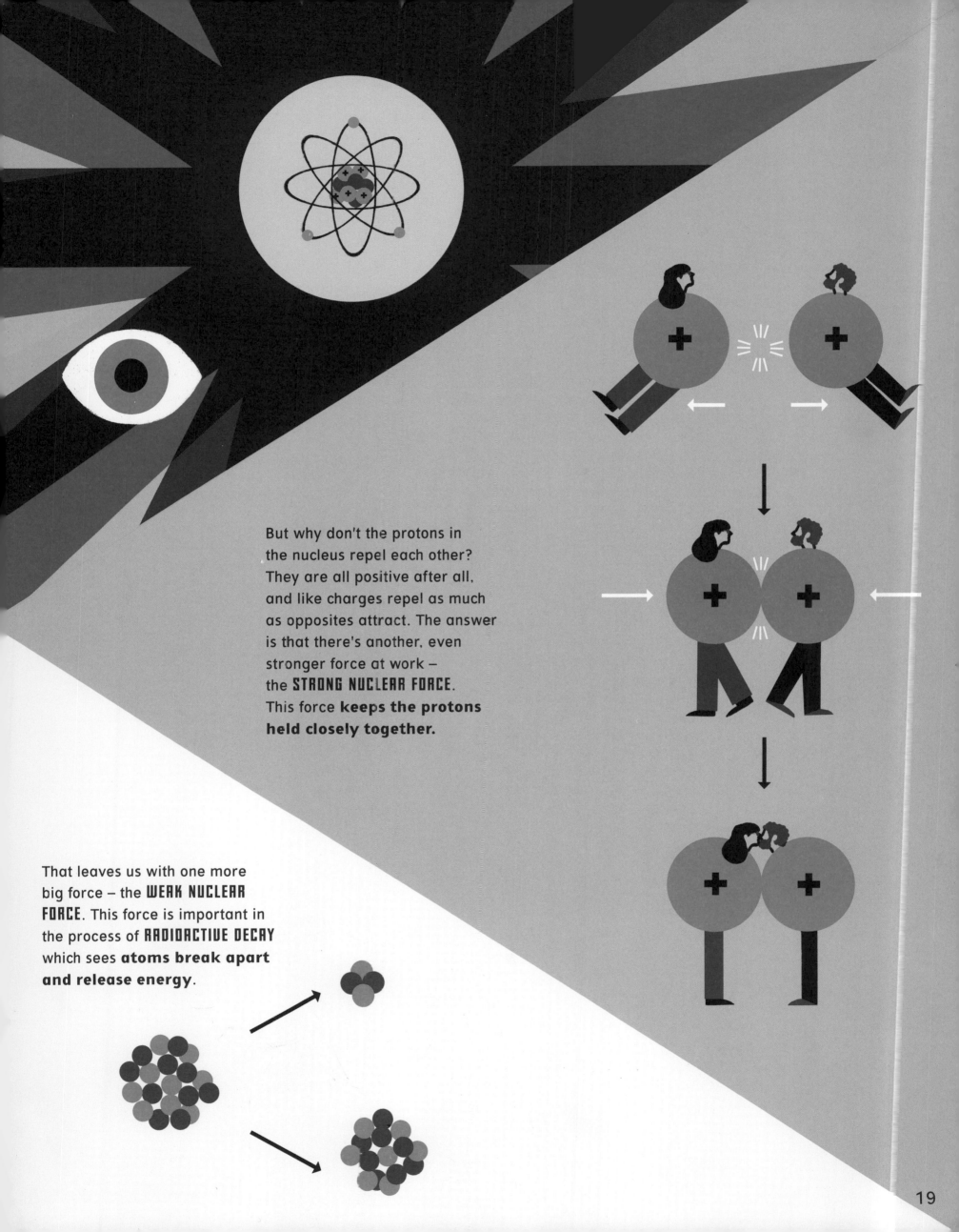

But why don't the protons in the nucleus repel each other? They are all positive after all, and like charges repel as much as opposites attract. The answer is that there's another, even stronger force at work – the **STRONG NUCLEAR FORCE**. This force **keeps the protons held closely together**.

That leaves us with one more big force – the **WEAK NUCLEAR FORCE**. This force is important in the process of **RADIOACTIVE DECAY** which sees **atoms break apart and release energy**.

Energy

Energy is something that's needed to perform a task. When you eat food your body turns some of it into energy to power your brain, heart and other organs. Burning a candle turns the chemical energy in the wax into heat and light energy. A camera turns light energy into electrical energy.

Energy is also part of the most famous equation in all of physics –

$$E = mc^2$$

Here, **E is energy**, **m is mass** and **c is the speed of light**. The brainchild of Albert Einstein, this equation says that energy and mass are the same thing and you can convert one into the other.

Energy is often transferred from one form to another but it can never be destroyed. Physicists call this the **LAW OF CONSERVATION OF ENERGY**. All types of energy fall into two groups – kinetic and potential. Any object in **motion** has **KINETIC** energy. This bike has kinetic energy.

POTENTIAL ENERGY

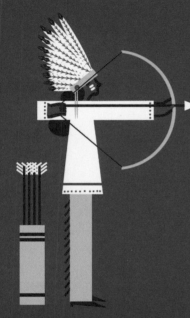

All objects have **POTENTIAL** energy. This is the energy that is **stored** within them. This bow has potential energy.

THE BIG BANG created a Universe initially filled with only energy, but various processes have turned some of that energy into the matter we see around us in the form of stars, planets and people.

What is Sound?

The world around us is a noisy place – birds singing, traffic rumbling, people talking and music blasting. All these sounds are caused by vibrations in the air around us.

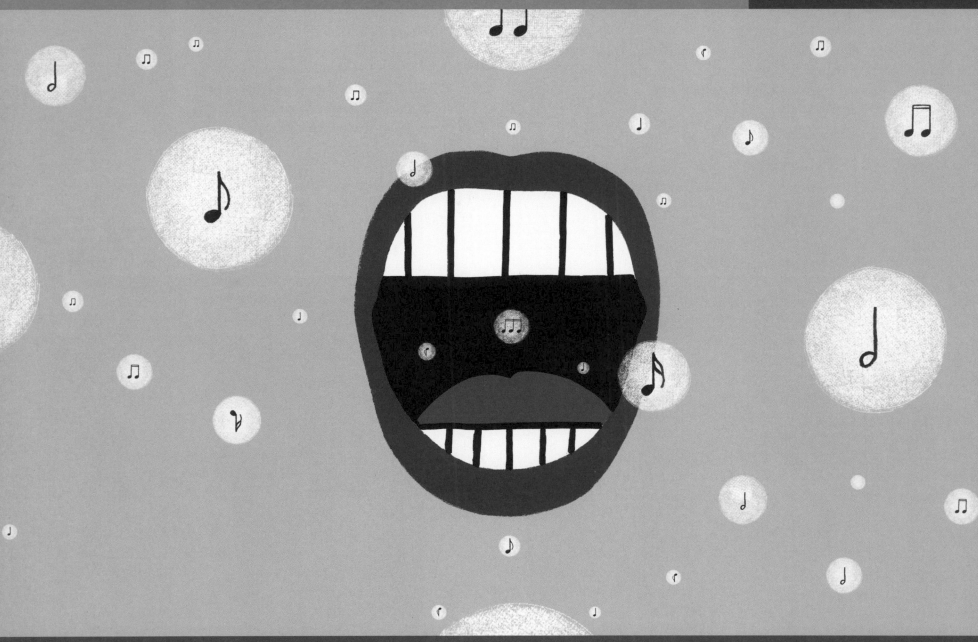

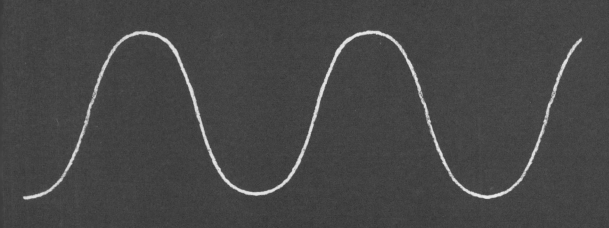

A speaker plays music by vibrating up and down, causing **AIR MOLECULES** nearby to **vibrate** too. Then their neighbours vibrate, and then their neighbours, until eventually the air molecules next to your ears are also dancing. This is how sound travels as a wave through the air. These waves travel around a million times slower than light travels, which is why you always see lightning before you hear thunder.

How do we Hear?

From beat boxers to Beethoven, we hear such rich and varied sounds thanks to our ears. The differences between them all come from the way microscopic hairs move deep inside our ears.

How the Ear Works:

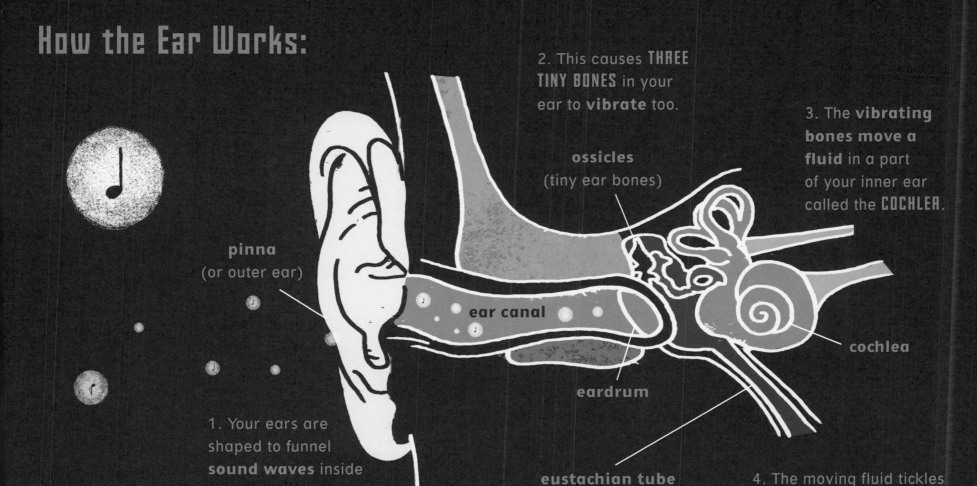

1. Your ears are shaped to funnel **sound waves** inside where they vibrate your **EARDRUM**.

pinna (or outer ear)

ear canal

2. This causes **THREE TINY BONES** in your ear to **vibrate** too.

ossicles (tiny ear bones)

3. The **vibrating bones move a fluid** in a part of your inner ear called the **COCHLEA**.

cochlea

eardrum

eustachian tube (sends signals to the brain)

4. The moving fluid tickles **TINY HAIRS** which **send nerve signals** to your brain. Here, the signals are interpreted as sounds.

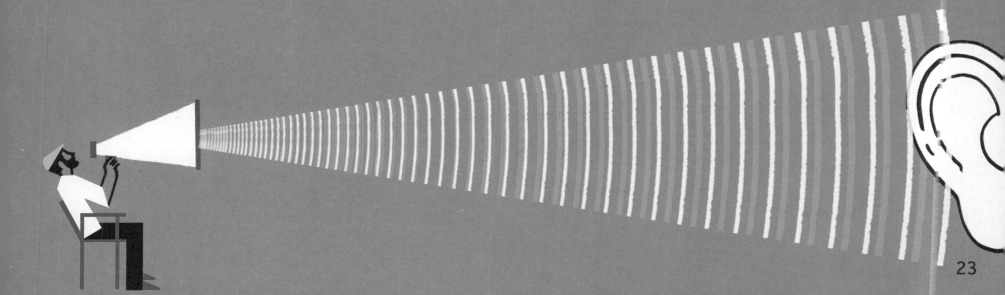

High and Low

There is a whole realm of sound above and below what we can hear. Some deep rumbles are **too low** to be heard [INFRASONIC] and other squeaks are too **high-pitched** [ULTRASONIC]. On average, humans can detect sounds that vibrate between 20 and 20,000 times a second. We measure the **frequency of sound vibrations** in HERTZ [Hz].

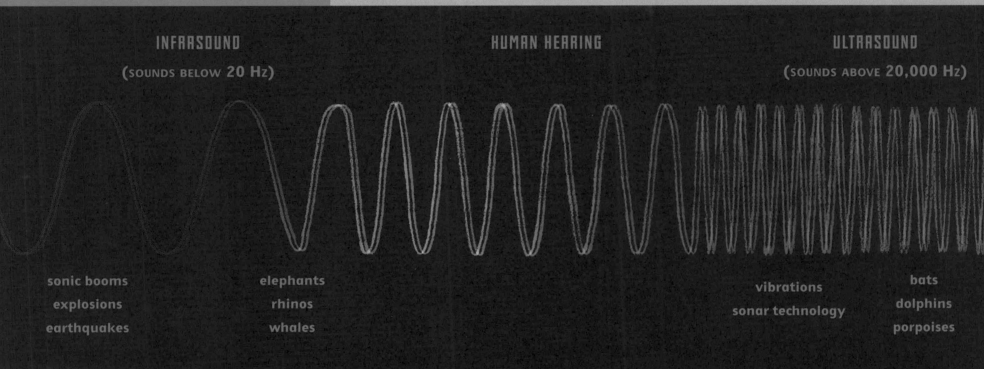

INFRASOUND
(SOUNDS BELOW **20 Hz**)

HUMAN HEARING

ULTRASOUND
(SOUNDS ABOVE **20,000 Hz**)

sonic booms
explosions
earthquakes

elephants
rhinos
whales

vibrations
sonar technology

bats
dolphins
porpoises

Bats can 'see' with their **ULTRASONIC** ears better than humans see with their eyes in daylight. They hunt in total darkness by scanning their environment with ultrasonic squeaks. **These squeaks vibrate 110,000 times a second**, and by swivelling their ears about, bats can close in on their prey.

Certain insects that can detect these sounds have evolved to stop them becoming dinner. Some moths, for example, close their wings and drop to the floor, while others fire out radar-jamming clicks.

Because light scatters quickly underwater, it is hard to see long distances. Instead, whales communicate using a range of **INFRASONIC** grunts, groans, snorts and barks. But they also do something quite remarkable – they sing. Male humpback whales sing tunes that can be heard on the other side of the ocean. Mastering their songs may get them a whale girlfriend!

Bats and toothed whales, such as dolphins and porpoises, use ultrasound **ECHOLOCATION** to find prey. They focus **high-pitched clicks** made inside their skulls into a beam of sound. When this 'sound ray' hits fish, part of it bounces back, allowing the hunters to pinpoint their prey. Humans have borrowed this trick to map the sea floor and find shoals of fish with sonar technology.

Pitch Perfect

Some sounds are pleasing to hear, but others cause you to put your hands over your ears. What makes a piano nicer to listen to than the rumble of traffic? It is all to do with harmonies.

Both traffic and a piano solo are several sounds of different frequencies all mixed up. Some musical notes sound good when played together, others are horrible. The ancient Greeks knew this and figured out that a note played with another double the frequency sounds harmonious. **Several harmonious notes** played together is known as a CHORD.

Musical instruments are able to create **NOTES – sounds with a constant frequency** – by making waves. Pluck a guitar string and it vibrates as a wave. Press a string down against the fret board of a guitar and you change the length of the string and the frequency of the vibrations. Blow into a wind instrument and the air inside it vibrates.

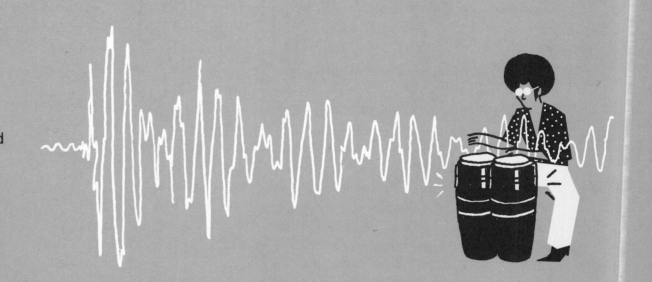

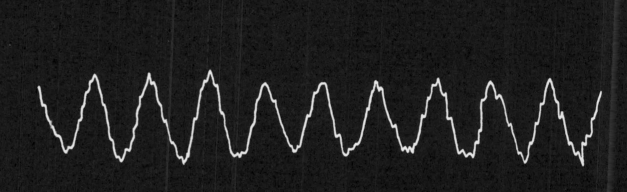

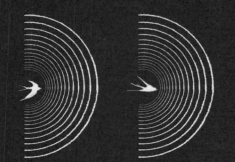

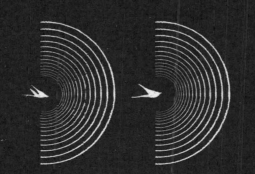

WHY DO BIRDS SING?

Have you ever listened to a bird call? As well as sounding pleasant, bird songs are also very important for the survival of birds – they can help to locate a mate or warn of danger. Scientists have discovered that hearing is so important to birds, they can regenerate destroyed cells in the ear and repair hearing loss. Studying how birds

Technically Speaking

The range of human language is amazing. As well as making over 500 different noises, we can speak at different volumes, from a whisper to a scream.

There are nearly seven thousand different languages spoken around the world. Although our voice box allows us to speak, the teeth, tongue and lips are also hugely important in making sounds. We combine them in different ways to create a whole multitude of noises. To test this, try saying the word 'top' in front of a mirror. Watch how your teeth and mouth move to create the sound. When you pronounce the letter 't', your teeth touch together, stopping the flow of air, whilst when you pronounce the letter 'p', your lips press together instead.

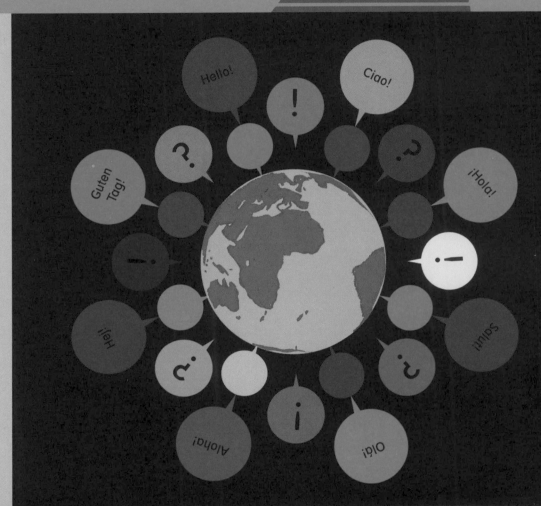

But not all human languages have words. The Hmong people of the Himalayas talk in whistles, whilst many of the Khoisan languages of Africa use clicks as well as words.

We can speak thanks to our **LARYNX** – or voice box – sitting at the top of the windpipe. If you touch your throat while talking you can feel it vibrating. It contains **folds of tissue** called **VOCAL CORDS** that vibrate as air passes through them. Men often have a pronounced 'Adam's apple' visible in their throat – this is their voice box sticking out slightly.

WHY CAN'T ANIMALS SPEAK?

Although animals are capable of making a whole range of sounds, they cannot speak in the same way as humans. Among other reasons, it is thought that this is because they cannot control the air entering and exiting their lungs like humans can. Animals need to take more breaths between each noise they make. Instead, they use a whole range of body and facial movements to communicate alongside sound.

How Loud is Loud?

We all know that some noises are louder than others – a cat purring is quieter than a drill, for example. Scientists measure the intensity of a sound on the **Decibel (dB) Scale**. It gets its name from **ALEXANDER GRAHAM BELL**, the inventor of the telephone, and from 'deci', the Latin word for a tenth.

The quietest sound you can hear is 0 dB. Each 10 dB jump up the scale represents a sound ten times more intense than the last. So a 20 dB sound is one hundred times more powerful than 0 dB (10 x 10), a 40 dB noise is 10,000 (10 x 10 x 10 x 10) times as intense. Mathematicians call this **a logarithmic scale**.

rocket
launching
180 dB

jet plane
taking off
140 dB

live rock
band
120 dB

motorcycle
100 dB

alarm clock
80 dB

conversation
60 dB

bird calls
40 dB

rustling
leaves
20 dB

pin drop
10 dB

The human ear is an amazing instrument capable of hearing sounds over a huge range. from rustling leaves (10 dB) to a rock concert (120 dB). Once sounds get to 130 dB they start to hurt your ears. At 160 dB they could well pierce your eardrum. This can lead to hearing loss. although it often repairs itself within a few weeks if left to heal.

Peace and Quiet

Imagine a place so quiet that you can hear the bones click in your joints, the blood coursing around your body and even your eyes moving in your skull. A place where even swallowing is deafening. This is exactly what happens inside anechoic chambers, the quietest places on the planet. 'ANECHOIC' is Latin for **'no echo'**.

The noise level inside Microsoft's anechoic chamber at its headquarters in Redmond. Washington, USA, is an unimaginable -20.6 dB. That's 100,000 times quieter than a whisper and way below what your ears can detect. The only sounds you'll pick up in there are ones inside your own body that are normally drowned out by the world around you.

To achieve such peace and quiet, the soundproofed room sits inside six layers of concrete. Bricks of noise-cancelling foam line the chamber's every surface. The majority of people find spending time in the chamber very uncomfortable and quickly ask to leave. Thankfully the room wasn't built for humans, but to test electronic equipment. Engineers are looking for tiny vibrations in computer components that might signal a faulty part.

It's impossible to find any natural spots on Earth that come close to the silence of the anechoic chamber, but there are still a few remote places in the world which have no sounds made by humans.

The Hoh Rainforest in Washington, USA, claims to have the 'quietest spot in the United States'. Located deep within the forest, a small red stone signifies 'One Square Inch of Silence'.

The Negev desert in Israel is reportedly so silent that you can hear your ears ring and the sand sing in the scorching heat.

Breaking the Sound Barrier

Just as a boat makes ripples as it moves through water, an object travelling through air creates waves around it. These waves travel at the **SPEED OF SOUND**, which is around **343 metres per second**.

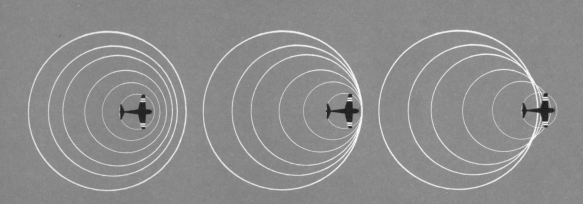

As the object itself approaches the speed of sound, the waves in front of it increasingly bunch up until they merge into **one giant shock wave** called a **SONIC BOOM**. For this reason, you cannot hear an object approaching you that is travelling faster than the speed of sound.

Humans are fascinated with making things go faster. Not long after the invention of planes, work began to make them fly even quicker. In 1947, US fighter pilot Chuck Yeager became the first person to break the sound barrier in a plane called the Bell X-1. He flew at 1,127 kilometres per hour! We call the speed of sound **Mach 1**, after **ERNST MACH** who conceived this measurement.

Since then, many planes have been able to fly even faster, thanks to improvements in design. Between 1976 and 2003, Air France and British Airways operated Concorde – a supersonic airliner that could travel from London, UK, to New York, USA, in under three hours at more than twice the speed of sound (Mach 2). The current airspeed record is held by a US spy plane, which can fly at 3.5 times the speed of sound!

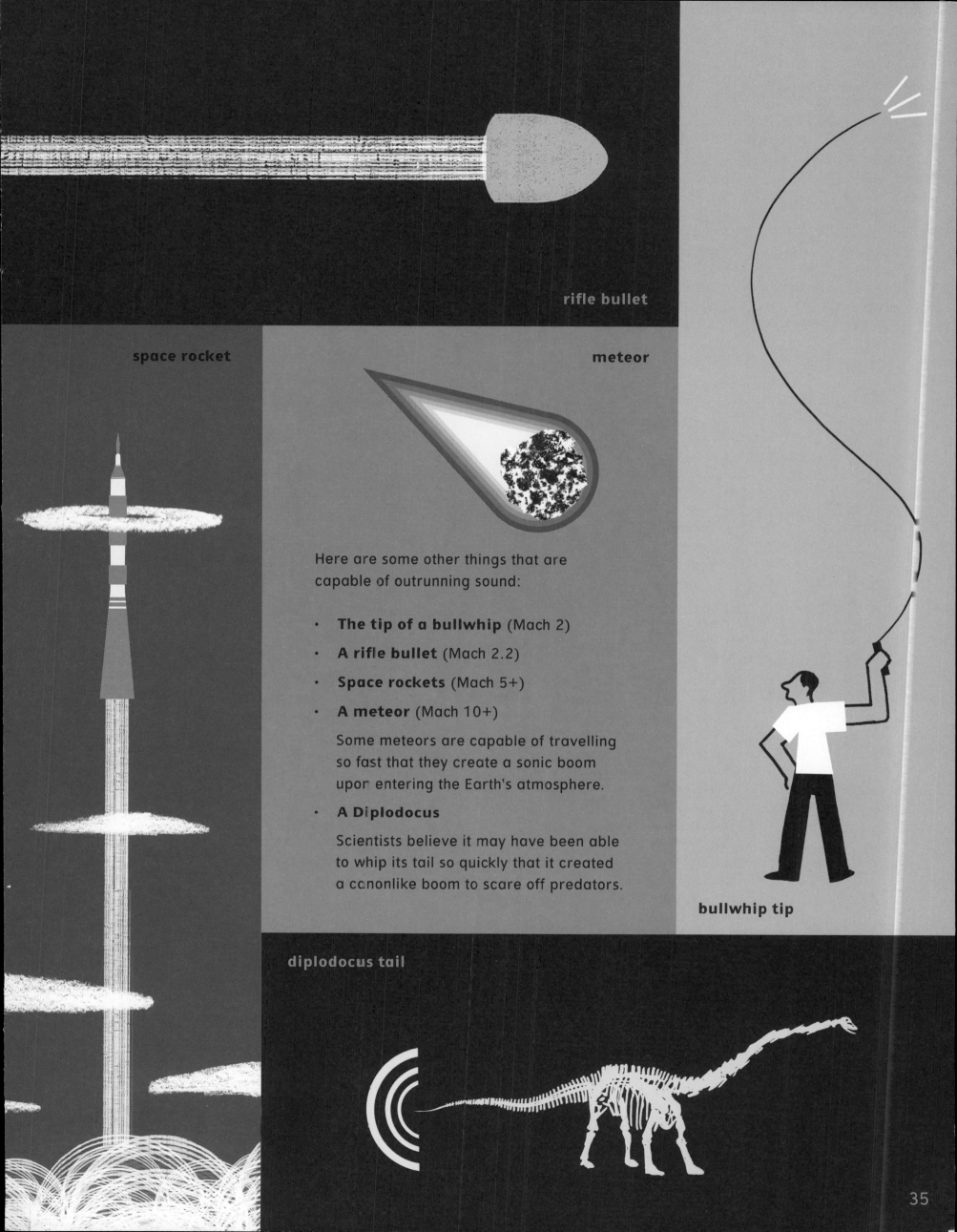

rifle bullet

space rocket

meteor

Here are some other things that are capable of outrunning sound:

- **The tip of a bullwhip** (Mach 2)
- **A rifle bullet** (Mach 2.2)
- **Space rockets** (Mach 5+)
- **A meteor** (Mach 10+)

  Some meteors are capable of travelling so fast that they create a sonic boom upon entering the Earth's atmosphere.

- **A Diplodocus**

  Scientists believe it may have been able to whip its tail so quickly that it created a canonlike boom to scare off predators.

bullwhip tip

diplodocus tail

Seismic Shakes

Suddenly, without warning, the ground starts to shake. Books fly off shelves as you huddle in a doorway for shelter. You're caught in the middle of an earthquake.

Scientists who study earthquakes are called **SEISMOLOGISTS**. They use seismic waves to understand what's going on deep inside the Earth and measure the strength of an earthquake on the **Richter scale**. The scale was developed by **CHARLES RICHTER** in 1935 and uses **numbers to represent the amount of energy released by earthquakes**. Each jump up the scale is 10 times more powerful than the last.

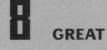

The Richter Scale

9 GREAT
Rare, but near total destruction of buildings, roads and bridges.

8 GREAT
Major destruction and death. Buildings and structures may collapse, bridges destroyed.

7 MAJOR
Quake can be detected all over the world.

6 MODERATE
Great damage around the epicentre. Cracks in the ground may appear and underground pipes may burst.

5 MODERATE
Damage caused to weaker buildings near the epicentre. Furniture may move and plaster could loosen from walls and ceilings.

4 SMALL
Some damage to buildings near the epicentre, including broken windows.

3 SMALL
People near the epicentre may feel this quake as vibrations.

2 MINOR
Smallest quake felt by people. Some hanging objects may swing.

1 INSIGNIFICANT
Humans cannot detect these quakes that happen almost daily.

These dramatic and violent events happen because the Earth's crust is not one solid surface. Instead, it is made up of a series of **interlocking jigsaw pieces** called TECTONIC PLATES. They float on top of a hot ocean of molten rock called magma. The Earth quakes when two plates rub against each other.

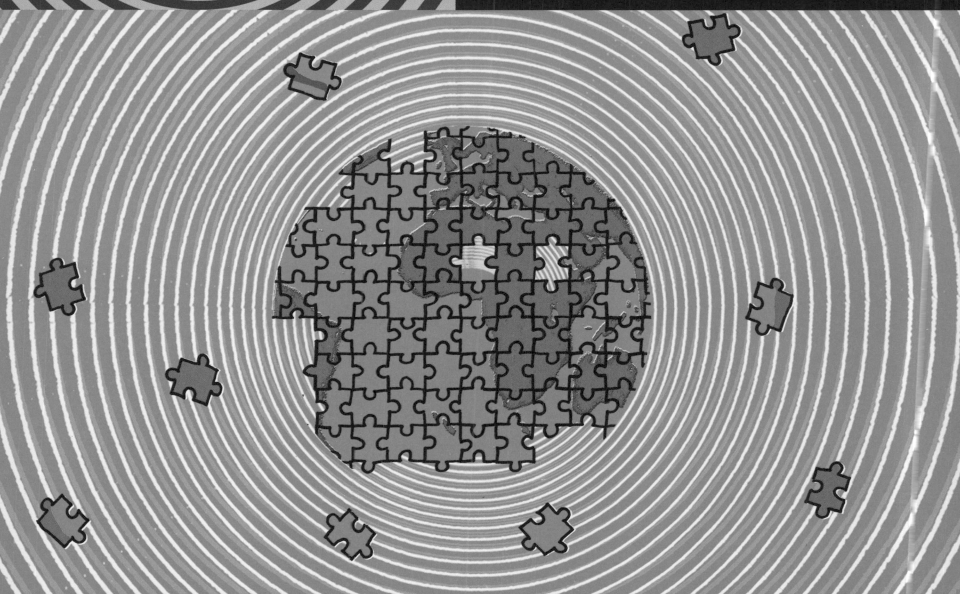

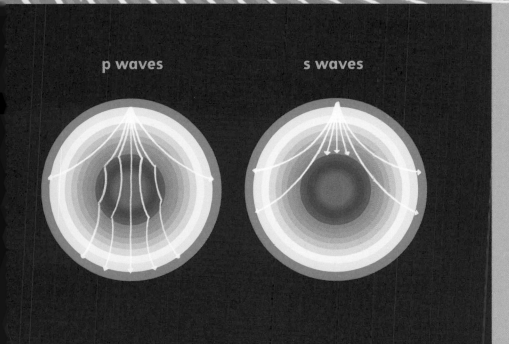

p waves   s waves

The energy from an earthquake travels through the Earth in the form of waves. Scientists split the waves into two types called P WAVES and S WAVES (Primary and Secondary). They **travel through the planet at different speeds and in different ways**.

P waves are most similar to sound waves and can travel all the way through the Earth. They can travel through both solids and liquids. However, the Earth's core stops S waves getting through. This is because it is made of molten liquid, and S waves can only travel through solids.

Noises of the World

Here are some of the noisiest and strangest
sounds ever recorded on Earth.

North
America

HOWLER MONKEY – 90 dB

The unmistakable call of this noisy
primate is generated by the hyoid
bone in their throat.

THE BLOOP, PACIFIC OCEAN
– 0-50 Hz

During the 1990s, strange noises
were picked up throughout the
Pacific Ocean. Hailed as one of
the loudest sounds ever recorded
underwater, some scientists think
it was caused by vibrations from
underwater volcanoes, but the
noises disappeared before we could
figure out what caused them. It is
known as The Bloop.

Pacific
Ocean

South
America

GREATER BULLDOG BAT
– 140 dB

Native to South America,
they're also known as
'fisherman bats' as they use
loud sounds to locate fish.

IGUAZU FALLS,
BRAZIL AND ARGENTINA –
100 dB

The largest waterfall system in
the world, water from the Iguazu
River rages over cliff-edges up to
82 metres high.

Southern
Ocean

Arctic
Ocean

TUNGUSKA, SIBERIA – 300 dB

In 1908, a meteor exploded above the ground in northern Russia. Luckily the area is deserted as the noise reached 300 dB.

Asia

Europe

PISTOL SHRIMP – 200 dB

These feisty creatures stun their prey with powerful jets of water from their claws, creating a shockwave louder than a gunshot.

KRAKATOA, INDONESIA – 172 dB

In 1883, this volcano erupted with such force that someone 160 kilometres away would have heard an enormous bang. Some say this was the loudest sound ever heard on Earth.

Africa

Pacific
Ocean

LION – 114 dB

As you may expect, the mighty roar of a lion is pretty loud and can be heard from 8 kilometres away.

Oceania

ICEBERG, ANTARCTICA
– 220 dB

An icequake occurs when an iceberg carves off a glacier. The resulting crack and boom can be louder than a rocket launching.

AUSTRALIA – 50-200 Hz

In the waters around Australia a strange quacking sound has been heard on and off since the 1960s. Locals have called it 'bio-duck'. Our best guess is that it comes from minke whales as they come up to the surface for air.

Antarctica

Sounds in Space

Sound cannot travel through space because there is no air to carry the vibrations. It's true what they say – in space, no one can hear you scream!

But astronomers can look at vibrating objects throughout the Universe and turn those vibrations into sound to help them understand what's going on. Stars like the Sun throb and pulse and **astronomers can use these vibrations to look deep inside** its layers. This is called ASTEROSEISMOLOGY.

As two black holes spin around each other, they **create vibrations** in the very fabric of space itself. Astronomers call them GRAVITATIONAL WAVES. The frequency of these waves increases as the black holes get nearer to each other. When they collide they produce a distinctive 'chirp'. Physicists have translated it into frequencies the human ear can hear.

The lowest note in the Universe is produced by a vibrating black hole in the Perseus cluster. It is a million billion times lower than the lowest note your ears can hear. It would sit 57 octaves below middle C on a piano keyboard. The left-hand end of a piano would have to be extended by 9 metres in order to play it!

What is Light?

Have you ever wondered what light actually is? It's a question that puzzled scientists for centuries. Physicists like Isaac Newton claimed it must be made of tiny, individual particles called corpuscles. But Dutch physicist Christiaan Huygens said it had to be a wave, like sound.

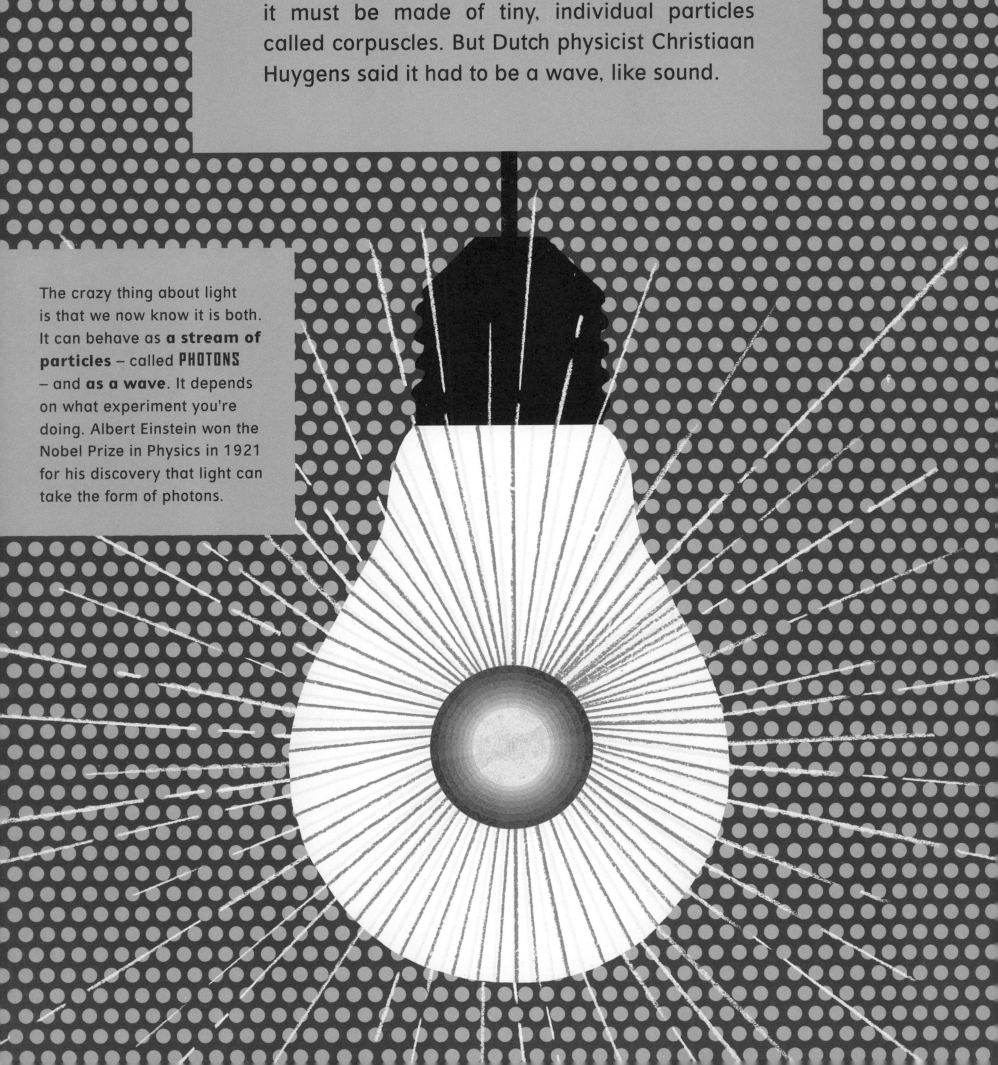

The crazy thing about light is that we now know it is both. It can behave as **a stream of particles** – called PHOTONS – and **as a wave**. It depends on what experiment you're doing. Albert Einstein won the Nobel Prize in Physics in 1921 for his discovery that light can take the form of photons.

How do we See?

We are able to see the world around us because light reflects off nearby objects and into our eyes.

How the Eye Works:

1. First, light travels through your **CORNEA** – **the thin transparent** layer at the front of your eye – before heading into your **PUPIL**.

2. Next, a **LENS focuses the light** onto a **projection screen** at the back of your eye called the **RETINA**, where the image is turned into electrical signals.

retina

cornea

pupil

lens

optic nerve

3. Your **OPTIC NERVE** sends those **signals to your brain** to make sense of.

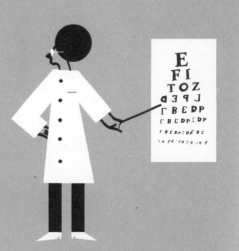

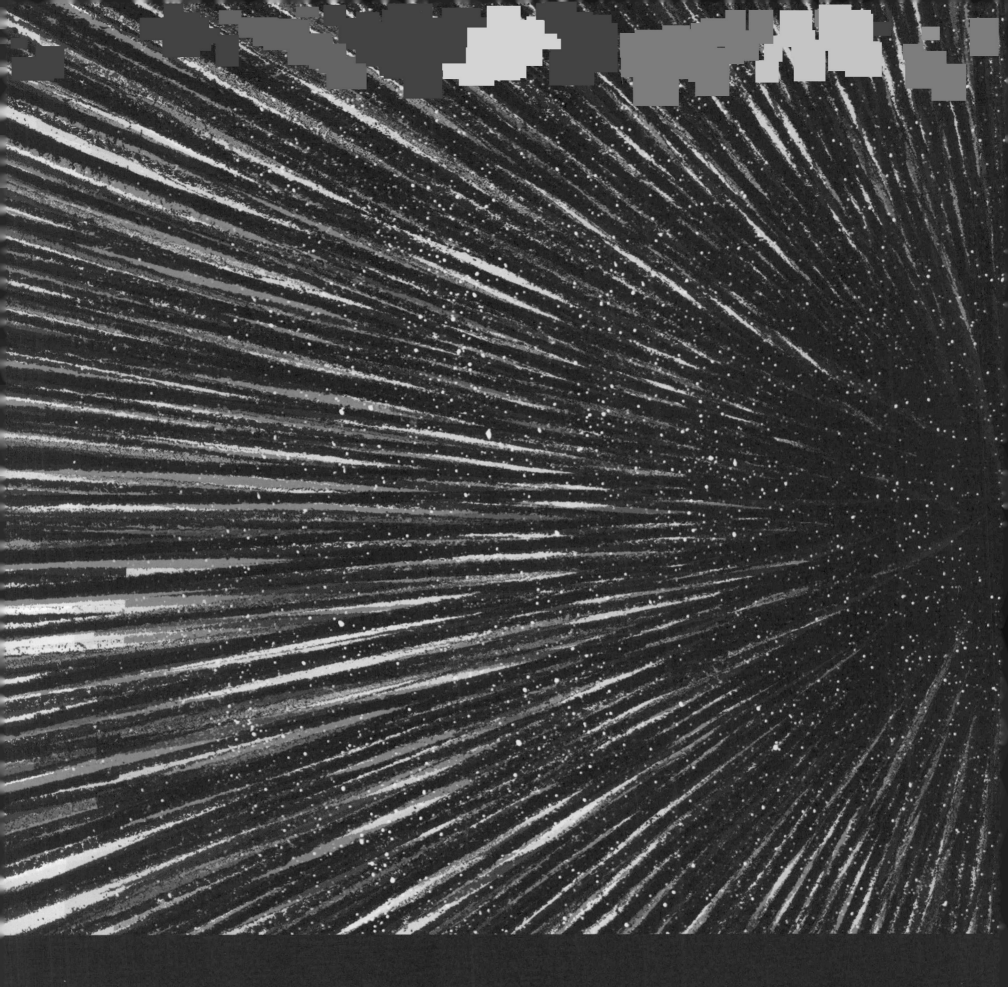

The Speed of Starlight

Light moves incredibly fast. Flick on a light switch and — BOOM — it instantly fills the room. As far as we know, light is the fastest thing in the Universe, but it is not infinitely fast.

Light travels at nearly 300,000 kilometres per second — about a million times faster than sound. At this pace, light would whizz around the Earth seven and a half times in one second. A **LIGHT YEAR** is **the distance light travels in a year**. This works

out at about 9,500,000,000,000 kilometres. This is a good way to measure the astronomical distances in space. The next-furthest star out from the Sun, Proxima Centauri, is just over four light years away, which means its light takes four

years to reach Earth. It would take 27,700 years to reach the centre of our Milky Way galaxy, 2,500,000 years to reach Andromeda (our nearest large galaxy) and a colossal 46,500,000,000 years to reach the furthest galaxies in the Universe.

SPEED OF LIGHT =
299,792,458 metres per second
Two hundred and ninety-nine million, seven hundred and ninety-two thousand, four hundred and fifty-eight metres per second

ONE LIGHT YEAR =
9,460,730,472,580,800 metres
Nine quadrillion, four hundred and sixty trillion, seven hundred and thirty billion, four hundred and seventy-two million, five hundred and eighty thousand, eight hundred metres

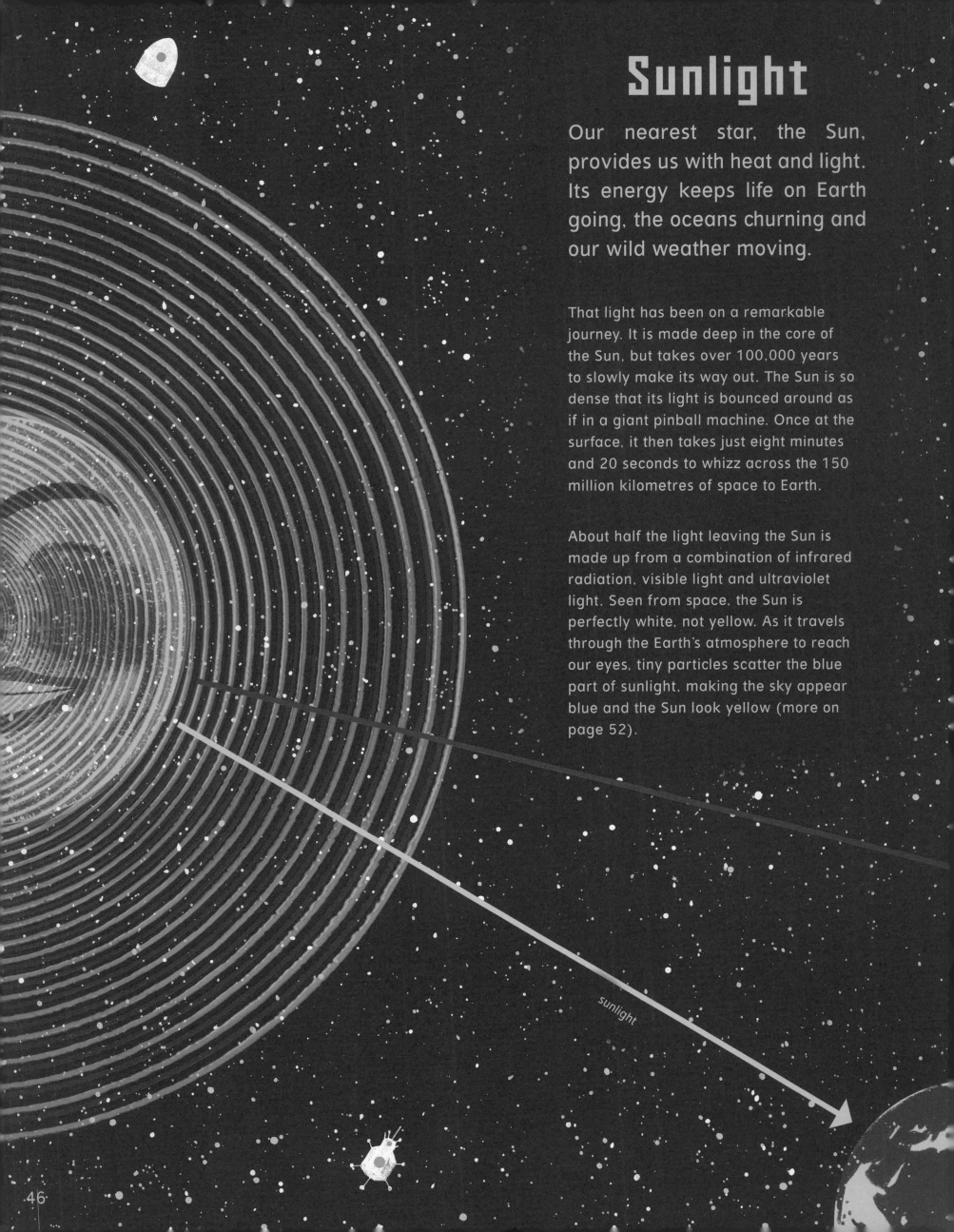

Sunlight

Our nearest star, the Sun, provides us with heat and light. Its energy keeps life on Earth going, the oceans churning and our wild weather moving.

That light has been on a remarkable journey. It is made deep in the core of the Sun, but takes over 100,000 years to slowly make its way out. The Sun is so dense that its light is bounced around as if in a giant pinball machine. Once at the surface, it then takes just eight minutes and 20 seconds to whizz across the 150 million kilometres of space to Earth.

About half the light leaving the Sun is made up from a combination of infrared radiation, visible light and ultraviolet light. Seen from space, the Sun is perfectly white, not yellow. As it travels through the Earth's atmosphere to reach our eyes, tiny particles scatter the blue part of sunlight, making the sky appear blue and the Sun look yellow (more on page 52).

sunlight

Moonlight

On a bright, moonlit night, the Moon looks as if it is shining with a pale, silver light. But the Moon does not glow — its light is reflected sunlight and even 'Earthshine' bouncing off its surface, exactly like a mirror.

The Moon is actually a pretty terrible mirror. Its surface is bumpy and a dark-grey colour. So, despite it being the brightest object in our night sky, the Moon only reflects just over a tenth of the light that hits it.

Light from the Sun travels across space to reach the Moon and Earth, but some of it is reflected back. We can only see the Moon because light from the Sun bounces off its surface, back to the Earth. If the Sun did not exist, we would never be able to see the Moon.

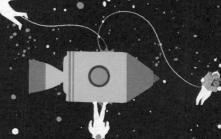

Sun's light reflected as 'moonlight'

Apollo astronauts have left reflectors on the Moon, which bounce light fired from lasers back to the Earth. Carefully measuring the time taken for the light to return shows that our Moon is drifting 3.8 centimetres further away from Earth every year — that's about as fast as your fingernails grow.

Sun's Core

The Sun is remarkable. It is the only object in the Solar System that is capable of making light on its own.

Every hour the Sun fuses 2.232 billion tonnes of protons (hydrogen) into 2.218 billion tonnes of helium. The missing 14 billion tonnes is turned into sunlight that pours out of the core. Even at this crazy rate, it will take the Sun billions more years to exhaust its supplies.

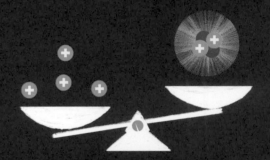

Sunlight is made deep in the heart of the Sun where gas is squashed together so fiercely that it becomes 13 times denser than lead. Temperatures in the core soar to a colossal 15 million degrees, as every second trillions upon **trillions of protons are forced together to create helium**. Astronomers call this process FUSION

Scientists have been trying to copy the Sun to make a fusion power station on Earth. The machines they use are called TOKAMAKS and temperatures inside can reach **100 million degrees** – hotter than the Sun's core.

Ferocious Flashes

If you thought the Sun's power was immense, it's nothing compared to the ferocious fury of a **GAMMA RAY BURST** (GRB).

In less than a minute, a GRB can release as much energy as the Sun will over its 10-billion-year lifetime. These brilliant flashes are created by either an exploding star or the cores of two stars smashing together after a dizzying death spiral.

GRBs belong to a group of objects studied by high energy astronomers. They explore the short-lived displays associated with black holes, neutron stars and supernova explosions – the Universe at its most extreme.

Some objects can get so bright that they can be seen more than halfway across the Universe, at distances where normal stars would be far too faint. In the middle of old galaxies, gargantuan black holes gorge on huge clouds of stars and gas, spewing out **vast quantities of X-rays and gamma rays**. Astronomers know these as **QUASARS** and **BLAZARS** and they can shine brighter than a thousand galaxies combined, even though a galaxy is made up of hundreds of billions of stars.

Making Food from Sunlight

Eating is one of the best things about being human – we have so many delicious things on offer. But it can also be a pain to have to remember to eat all the time. What if we could use our bodies to make our own food from scratch, whenever we wanted? Well, that's exactly what plants do. It is called **PHOTOSYNTHESIS**.

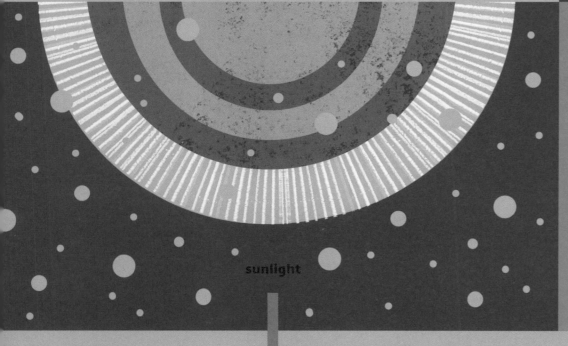

sunlight

When you eat fruit and vegetables, the energy from their sugar passes on to you. So energy moves from the Sun to plants, then animals and then you in a series of steps which scientists call a **FOOD CHAIN**. Many **overlapping food chains in an ecosystem are known as a FOOD WEB**. The first link in a chain is always the Sun – so even when you eat a hamburger what you're really eating is repackaged solar energy!

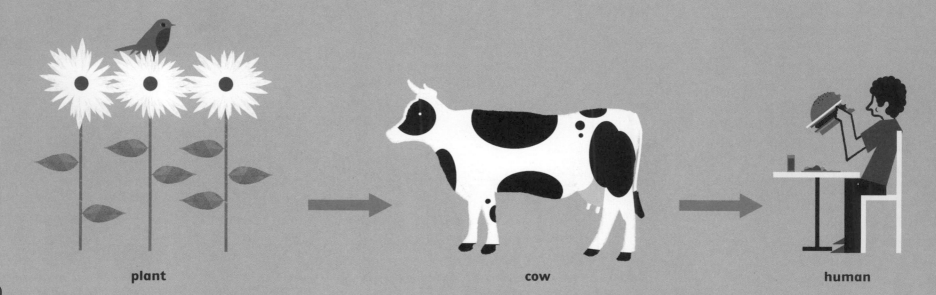

plant   cow   human

Inside a Plant Cell

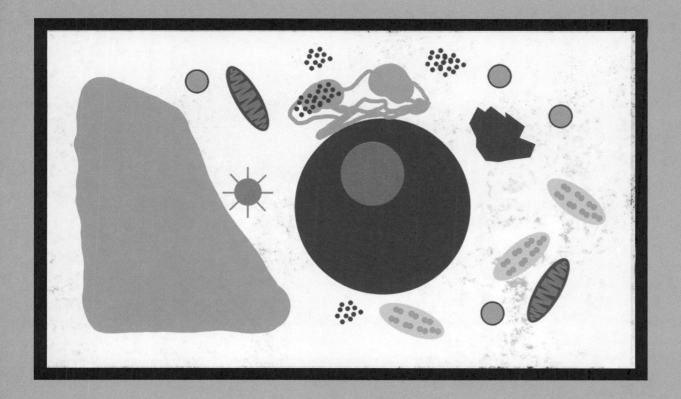

Plants use a green chemical called **CHLOROPHYLL** to **absorb sunlight** in their leaves. They combine this with water and carbon dioxide from the air to create oxygen and sugar. They use the sugar as food and release the oxygen into the atmosphere.

Photosynthesis

The **process in which plants create food and oxygen** is called **PHOTOSYNTHESIS**.

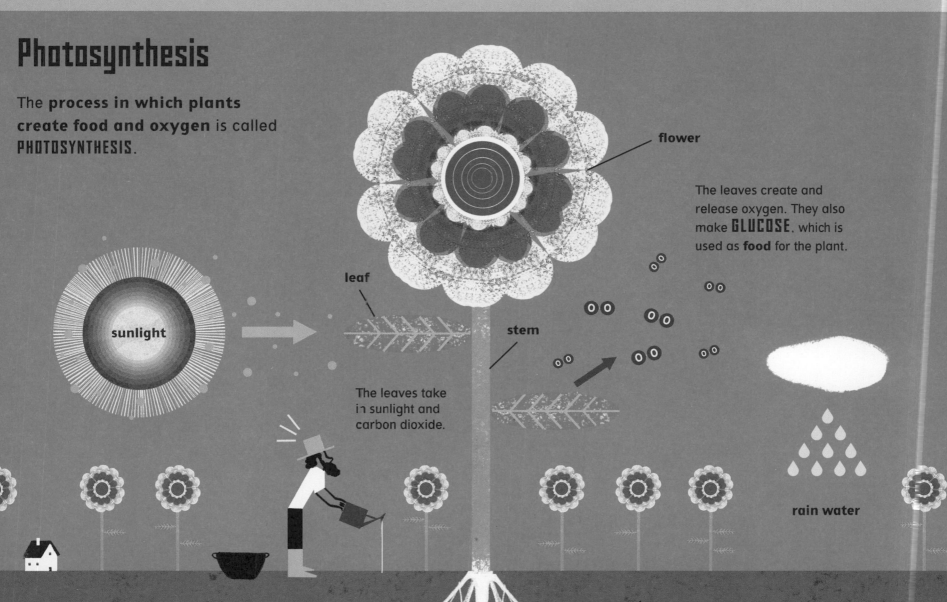

sunlight

leaf

flower

stem

The leaves create and release oxygen. They also make **GLUCOSE**, which is used as **food** for the plant.

The leaves take in sunlight and carbon dioxide.

rain water

roots

The roots absorb water and nutrients from the soil.

Why is the Sky Blue?

You can think of light as a wave, much like a wave on the ocean. The **distance over which a wave repeats** is called its **WAVELENGTH**. Red light has a much longer wavelength than blue light.

The different colours of sunlight are scattered by air molecules as they enter the Earth's atmosphere. How much a colour gets scattered depends on its wavelength.

Imagine that light is taking footsteps across the sky. **RED LIGHT**, with its **long wavelength**, has big footsteps like a giant so it can easily walk over most of the air molecules.

However, **BLUE LIGHT** can only take much **shorter** steps and so it gets scattered the most. When you look up at the sky in the middle of a clear day most of the scattered light that hits your eyes is blue.

At sunrise and sunset, however, the light from a low-down Sun has to travel through a lot more atmosphere to reach your eyes. Only the light with the biggest footsteps – the longest wavelength – can make it through all that gas. That's why the sky appears red at these times.

Splitting the Rainbow

With the smell of rain still in the air, the Sun emerges from the clouds and a glorious rainbow stretches across the sky. These vivid, colourful arches are caused by sunlight entering water droplets.

You can only see a rainbow if the Sun is behind you because the light goes in front of the raindrop, hits the back and then returns towards you.

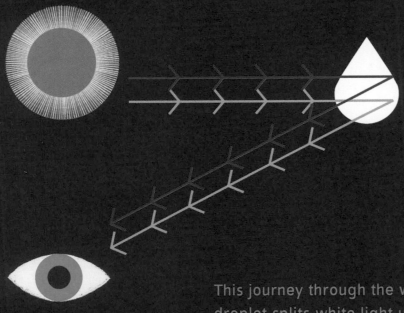

This journey through the water droplet splits white light up into its seven colours: red, orange, yellow, green, blue, indigo and violet.

There is often a second, fainter rainbow, too. Look closely and you'll spot that its colours are reversed. The sky is also noticeably darker between the two rainbows. This **dingy patch** is called ALEXANDER'S DARK BAND.

We're so used to seeing rainbows as arcs, but that's because the ground normally blocks out the rest of the circle. Mountaineers and pilots can sometimes see a complete, circular rainbow. Earth isn't the only planet with rainbows either – astronomers have spotted one on Venus and think they might also exist on Saturn's largest moon, Titan.

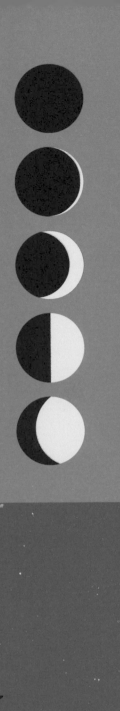

Spectacular Eclipses

The night sky is full of beautiful objects, but few events rival the jaw-dropping spectacle of a **SOLAR ECLIPSE**. The **Moon creeps in front of the Sun, blocking out most of its light** and causing temperatures to drop. Animals that were busy going about their business go quiet in confusion, creating an eerie silence.

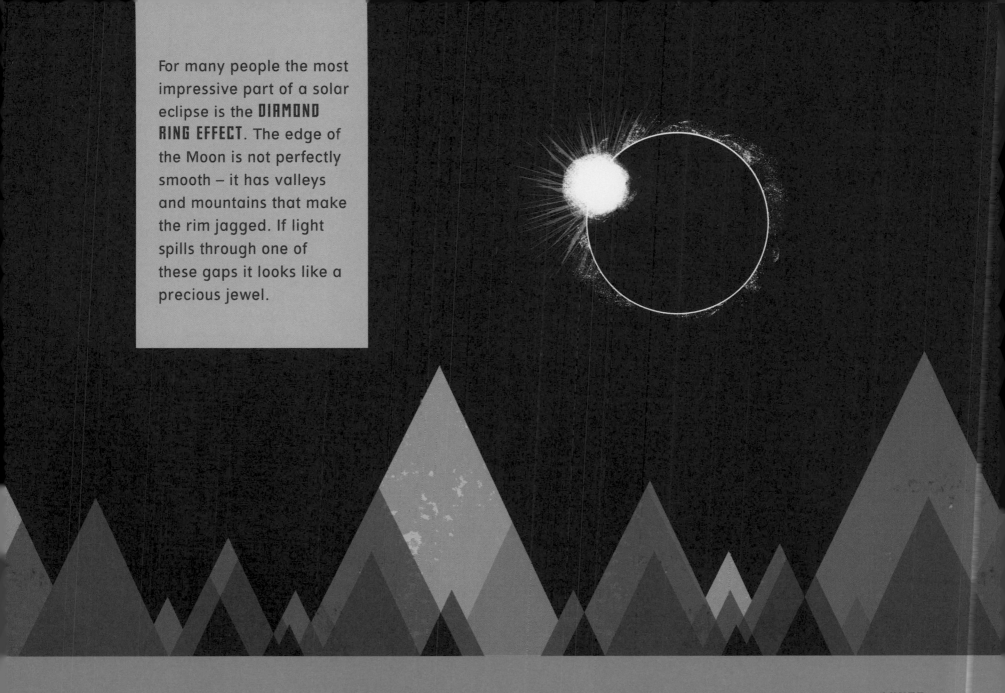

For many people the most impressive part of a solar eclipse is the **DIAMOND RING EFFECT**. The edge of the Moon is not perfectly smooth – it has valleys and mountains that make the rim jagged. If light spills through one of these gaps it looks like a precious jewel.

The other main type of eclipse is a **LUNAR ECLIPSE**. We get these when **the Moon moves behind the Earth and into the shadow** we cast into space. Normally this would stop any sunlight reaching the Moon at all. But the atmosphere above our heads is able to bend the red part of the colour spectrum around our planet. This turns the Moon a spooky, deep blood red colour.

Sun

Earth

Moon

Nature's Light Displays

The natural world is capable of putting on displays of light as good as any fireworks display. People living close to the Earth's poles are often treated to the beauty of AURORAE – also known as the **Northern** and **Southern Lights**. They are caused when atoms in our atmosphere receive extra energy from space and give out light. You can hear clapping, clicking and popping noises too, as these curtains of light dance above your head.

Several times a year we are treated to glorious **METEOR SHOWERS** – bursts of shooting stars that tear across the sky. They are not stars at all, but **tiny grains of space dust** burning up high in our atmosphere.

Creatures in the ocean such as jellyfish and squid are good at making impressive light shows as well. This is called **BIOLUMINESCENCE**. Glowing algae once saved the life of astronaut Jim Lovell, the commander of the Apollo 13 mission, when he was a fighter pilot. His night navigation equipment failed and he couldn't find his aircraft carrier – that is until he saw the bioluminescent algae being churned up by the ship. He followed the glowing water all the way to a safe landing.

Telescopes

The best way to think about telescopes is as giant light buckets. Imagine that the starlight falling to the Earth is rain. If you want to collect more rain you need a bigger bucket. Our eyes are pretty small and so they can only collect so much light on their own. That's why we build bigger buckets (telescopes). It means we can see faint-looking objects that are further away.

Telescopes come in two main types —
REFLECTORS (which use **mirrors**) and
REFRACTORS (which use **lenses**). The
biggest telescopes in the world are all
reflectors as it is easier and cheaper
to build big mirrors.

It is also very important where a telescope is
built. It needs to be put somewhere where the
weather is really good so there aren't too many
cloudy nights. The atmosphere can make stars
blurry, so it also needs to be built somewhere high
up so that there is as little air as possible to look
through. One of the world's best telescopes, the
wonderfully-named **VERY LARGE TELESCOPE [VLT]**,
sits 2,600 metres up in the bone dry Atacama
Desert in Chile.

61

Invisible Rays

Just as there are sounds too low and high for our ears to hear, there is light too low or high in frequency for us to see. In fact, most of the light around us is invisible. Scientists have invented some clever ways for us to see what our eyes cannot.

Below the red end of the colour spectrum we venture into infrared and then journey on to low frequency microwaves and radio waves. These all have long wavelengths. Above the violet, sits ultraviolet and then X-rays and gamma rays. These have much shorter wavelengths. This **complete set of light rays** is called the ELECTROMAGNETIC SPECTRUM.

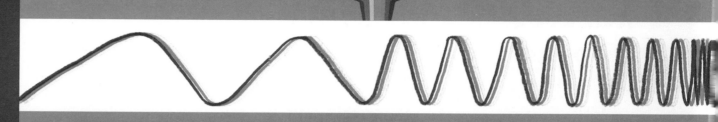

radio waves	microwaves	infrared	ultraviolet	X-rays	gamma rays

The Universe is playing a symphony using all of these invisible rays and our eyes can only pick up on a few notes. Black holes churn out X-rays, colliding neutron stars flash bright in gamma rays and pulsating stars beam out radio waves. If we restricted ourselves to just the light our eyes can see we'd really be missing out, so we build telescopes to see the light we can't.

Some parts of the electromagnetic spectrum – such as X-rays – don't make it to the ground, so we have to launch telescopes into space if we want to detect them. Only visible light and radio waves make it down here through our atmosphere and magnetic field.

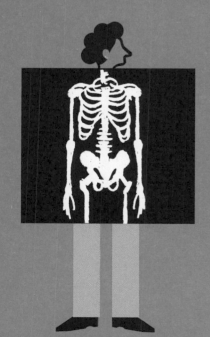

visible light

radio waves

In the Beginning

The **oldest light in the Universe** is called the COSMIC MICROWAVE BACKGROUND [CMB]. To start with, the Universe was too jam-packed for light to travel very far. But, 380,000 years after the Big Bang, the expansion of the Universe meant there was suddenly enough space for light to flood out freely. Scientists discovered microwaves flowing from every direction in space, which they believe came from one source.

That makes the CMB the equivalent of the Universe's baby picture. If the Universe were a 40-year-old, the CMB is a snapshot of what it was like when it was just 10 hours old!

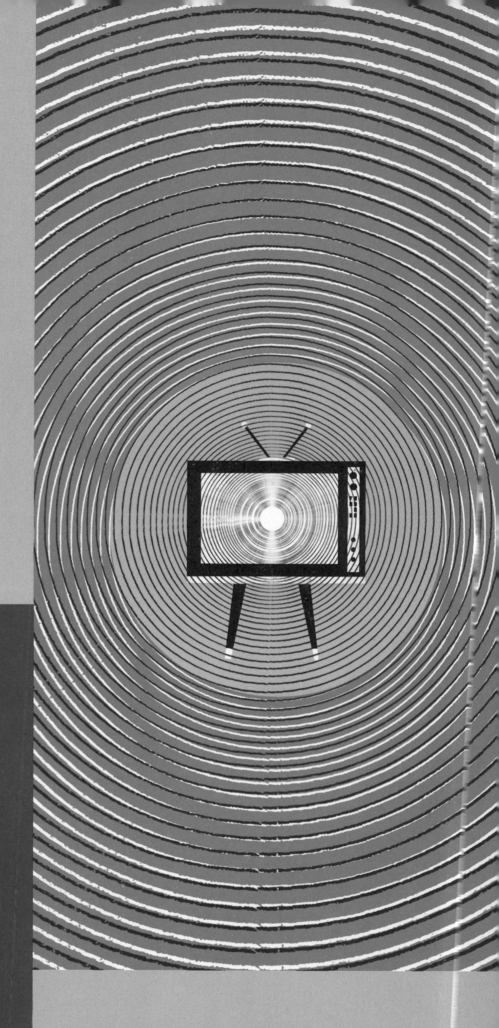

The CMB was originally discovered by accident in the 1960s by two American astronomers – **Arno Penzias** and **Robert Wilson**. They detected a hum in their radio telescope that they couldn't get rid of. At one point they thought it might be due to poo from pigeons roosting in their antenna – but the signal remained even after the pigeons had been evicted. What they were really picking up was the **afterglow of the Big Bang.**

You, too, can tune into the CMB using an analogue TV or radio. One per cent of the crackling interference you get between stations is due to this ancient light from the birth of our Universe.

Searching for Aliens

It's arguably the biggest of all questions –
are we alone in the Universe? To find out,
astronomers have been scanning space,
searching for planets around other stars.

Welcome

Alien planets are too small, dim and
far away to be seen directly. Instead,
astronomers have clever ways to tell if
one is there. Scientists don't just look for
aliens, they listen out for them with radio
telescopes too. For decades they have been
scanning the skies for any messages from
ET, but so far they haven't heard anything.

If a planet moves in front of its star,
then we see the star get a little dimmer.
Planets also have a small gravitational
pull on their star. This causes the star to
wobble, which we can spot through clues
in the starlight we see.

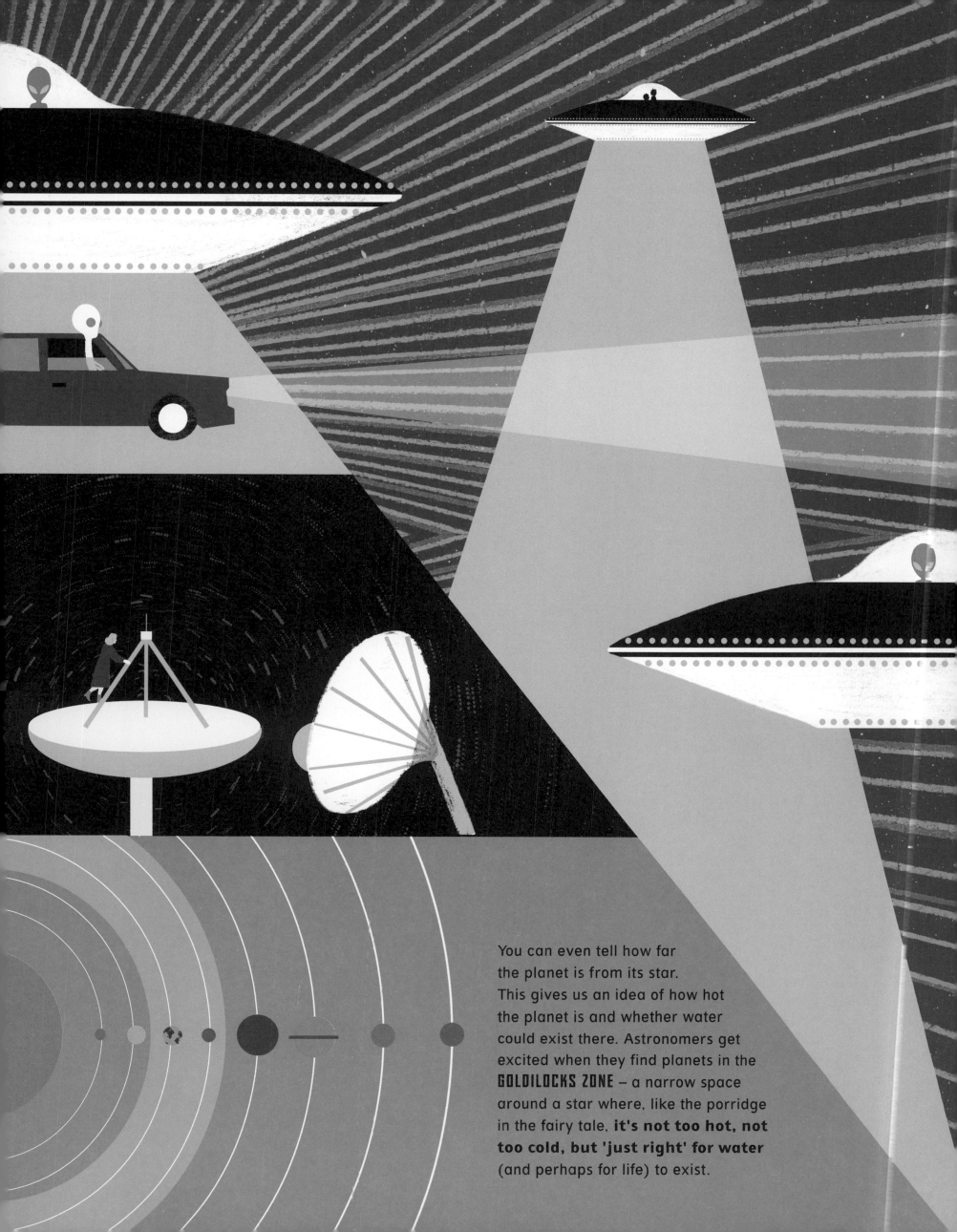

You can even tell how far the planet is from its star. This gives us an idea of how hot the planet is and whether water could exist there. Astronomers get excited when they find planets in the **GOLDILOCKS ZONE** — a narrow space around a star where, like the porridge in the fairy tale, **it's not too hot, not too cold, but 'just right' for water** (and perhaps for life) to exist.

How Old are Stars?

How do you even begin to work out the age of a star and what it's made of? After all, they're so far away that you can't go there. Even if you could, the temperatures would be too extreme to take a sample – even in a spacesuit, you couldn't get closer than five million kilometres to the Sun before becoming toast. Astronomers have to think differently.

Stages of a Star

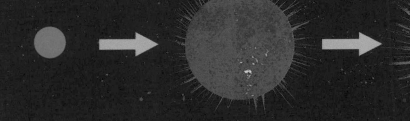

Much like humans, stars also have life cycles. Yellow stars like our Sun will stay that way for billions of years before cooling and expanding into a red giant. Blue stars will keep cooling and expanding before eventually collapsing, causing them to explode in an event known as a supernova (more on pages 74-75).

To measure the age of a star, astronomers have to think smart and use the only thing they have – starlight. If you pass starlight through an instrument called a **SPECTROMETER** – which is a bit like a prism – you can **split the light** into the familiar spectrum of rainbow colours. Look carefully, however, and you'll notice that some hues are missing. That's because different chemical elements in the star swallowed that colour of light before it could head out into space. So this spectrum acts like a barcode, telling us exactly what a star is made of.

This gives astronomers a neat way to age a star. In the early Universe, the only ingredients around for making stars were hydrogen and helium. But as the Universe matured, more and more elements were added to the pot. So a very old star is made of just hydrogen and helium. Younger stars have a much richer barcode with more missing colours.

69

The Dark Universe

The Universe is like an iceberg – the bit we can see is only a small part of what's really there. In the last few decades astronomers have realised that they don't know what the rest is made of.

As we learnt on page 18, everything around us is made of atoms. However, it seems that's not the case with space. Atoms only make up 5 per cent of the Universe. The rest is split between two shadowy and mysterious substances called dark matter and dark energy.

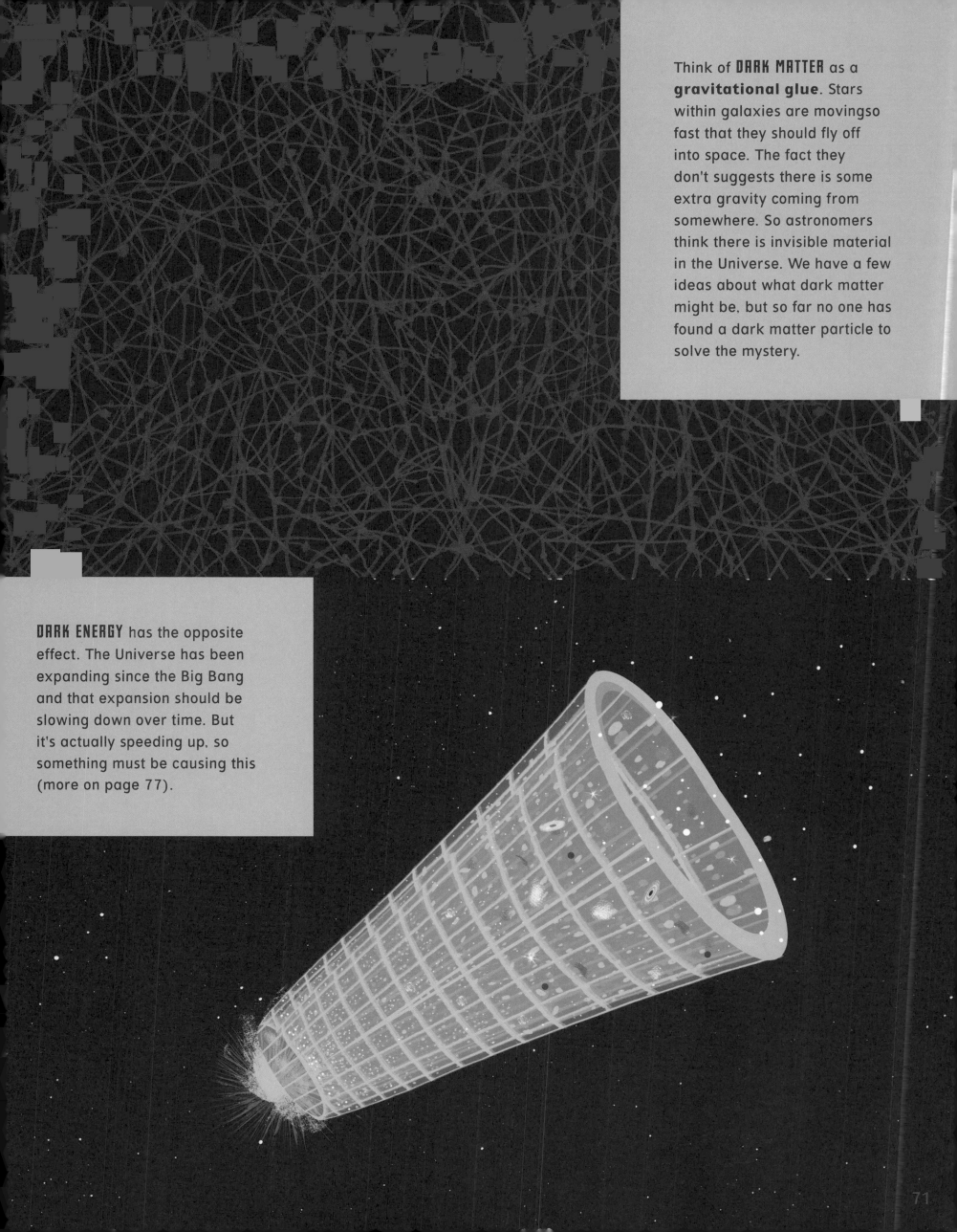

Think of **DARK MATTER** as a **gravitational glue**. Stars within galaxies are movingso fast that they should fly off into space. The fact they don't suggests there is some extra gravity coming from somewhere. So astronomers think there is invisible material in the Universe. We have a few ideas about what dark matter might be, but so far no one has found a dark matter particle to solve the mystery.

DARK ENERGY has the opposite effect. The Universe has been expanding since the Big Bang and that expansion should be slowing down over time. But it's actually speeding up, so something must be causing this (more on page 77).

Black Holes

You can only see these words because light is bouncing off the page and entering your eyes. Imagine instead that the book swallowed any light that hit it. You'd be left in the dark as to what's inside. That's exactly what's happening with a black hole.

When a really big star dies it warps the space around it to such extremes that any light trying to escape ends up curving back in. To successfully get away from a black hole you need to travel faster than the speed of light and we know that's not possible (see page 44).

So what happens to you if you're unlucky enough to fall in to one? The answer is not good. The difference in gravity between your feet and your head would be greater than the bonds between your atoms – which means you'd **get stretched and pulled apart**. Physicists have a word for this process – **SPAGHETTIFICATION**. At the moment no one knows what would happen to your spaghettified atoms at the bottom of the black hole.

Anything can be a black hole if it is compact enough. Shrink the Earth down to the size of your thumbnail and light wouldn't be able to escape. This is because it would become too dense for anything to break free of its gravitational field.

Standard Candles

Two stars are locked in a gravitational dance when the life of one is extinguished. All that's left is a **small core** the size of the Earth called a **WHITE DWARF**. The white dwarf then starts gorging on its neighbour, stealing gas and bulking itself up. But it gets too greedy, eats too much and explodes with unimaginable force and searing light that can be seen halfway across the Universe.

These cataclysmic events – called type Ia supernovas – allow astronomers to measure the distances to far dway galaxies. **White dwarfs explode when they have roughly the same amount of material as 1.4 Suns.** This is called the **CHANDRASEKHAR LIMIT** after the 19-year-old Indian astrophysicist who calculated that number during a three-week boat journey to Europe in 1930.

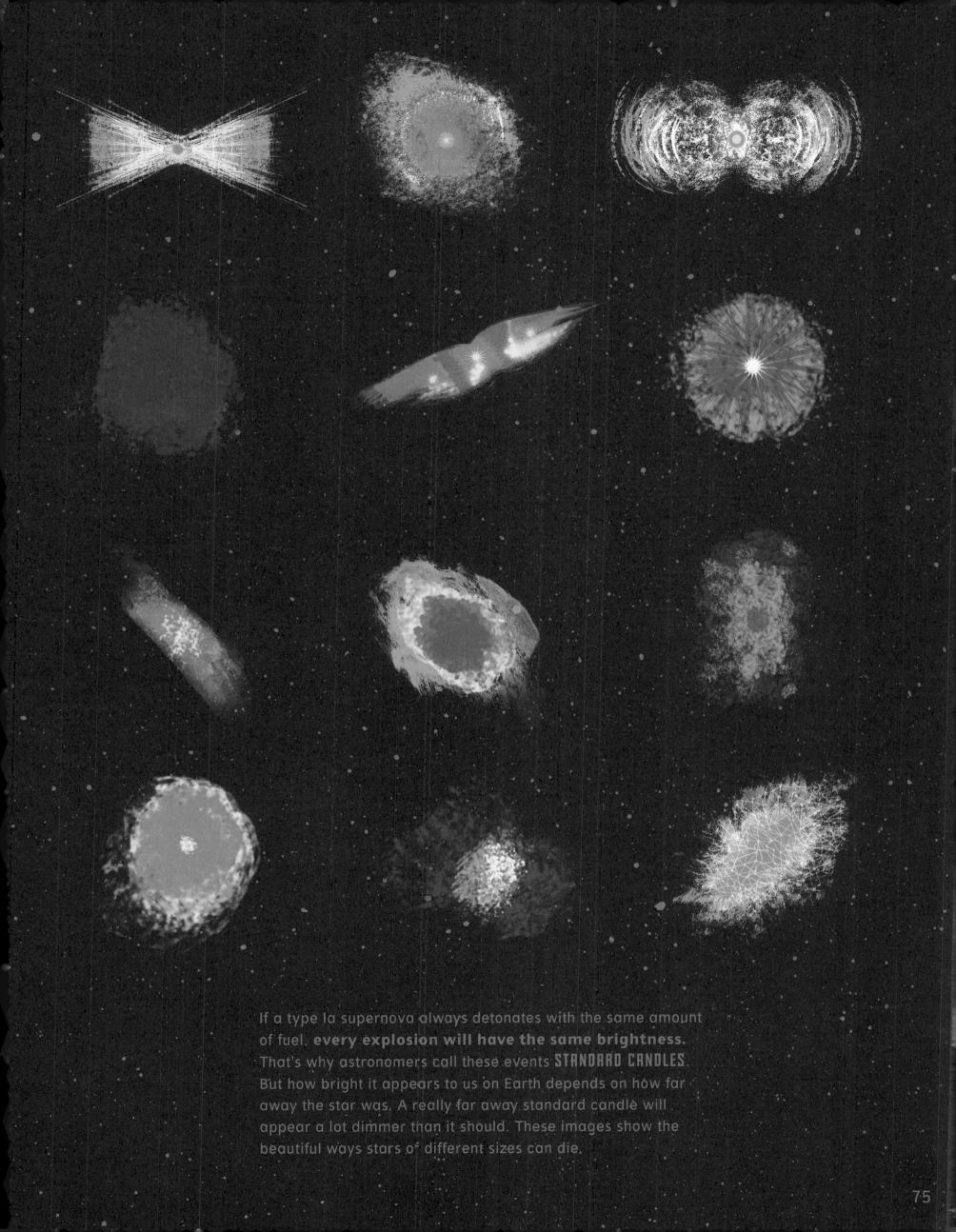

If a type Ia supernova always detonates with the same amount of fuel, **every explosion will have the same brightness**. That's why astronomers call these events STANDARD CANDLES. But how bright it appears to us on Earth depends on how far away the star was. A really far away standard candle will appear a lot dimmer than it should. These images show the beautiful ways stars of different sizes can die.

The Expanding Universe

Have you ever heard an ambulance race by on the way to an emergency? Did you notice that **the sound of the siren changed** as it tore past you? This is called the **DOPPLER EFFECT** and astronomers used the same idea to discover how our Universe got started.

As an ambulance hurtles towards you, the sound waves it emits get squashed together – their wavelength goes down. Yet once it rockets away from you it begins to stretch the sound waves out. This shifts the sound of the siren to a lower pitch.

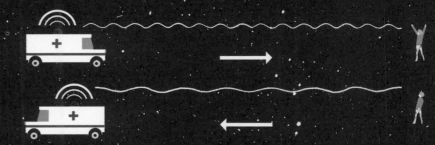

Light is a wave too, so the same thing happens to moving light sources, except it is not the pitch that changes but the colour. Light sources **approaching** us appear bluer [BLUESHIFT] and those running **away** from us appear redder [REDSHIFT].

In the 1920s, astronomers noticed that the light from almost every galaxy in the Universe is redshifted – they're all moving away from us. This made them realise our Universe must be expanding and that expansion started with **a big bang nearly 14 billion years ago.** This is known as the BIG BANG THEORY. Dark energy is now making this expansion speed up and it remains one of the Universe's greatest mysteries.

Aside from dark energy, there is much more to be explored. We have yet to discover if life exists on other planets, or indeed what happens at the bottom of a black hole. Who knows what we might discover next and where it may lead us?